ANIMAL
STORIES

FRANKLIN WATTS
LONDON • SYDNEY

First published in the UK in 2014 by Franklin Watts

Franklin Watts
338 Euston Road
London NW1 3BH

Franklin Watts Australia
Level 17/207 Kent Street
Sydney, NSW 2000

Dewey classification: 398.2'454

A CIP catalogue record for this book is available from the British Library.

ISBN: 978 1 4451 3236 5

Franklin Watts is a division of Hachette Children's Books, an Hachette UK company.
www.hachette.co.uk

TEN OF THE BEST MYTHS ANIMAL STORIES
was produced for Franklin Watts by
David West Children's Books, 6 Princeton Court, 55 Felsham Road, London SW15 1AZ

Designed and illustrated by David West
Contributing editor: Steve Parker

Printed in China

THE STORIES

Anansi the Spider

This is the story of how Anansi the trickster came to own all of the stories in the whole world.

Long ago, all the stories in the world belonged to the sky god, Nyame. Anansi the Spider had long wanted to own them and one day he offered to buy them.

"I am happy to sell you my stories, Anansi, but my price is high," said Nyame. "You must bring me Mmoboro the hornet, Onini the python, and also Osebo the leopard."

Anansi set to work straight away. First he approached the hornet's nest carrying an empty **gourd** with a small hole in it. Sprinkling water over the nest, he shouted: "It is raining and your fragile nest will soon be destroyed! Quick, fly into this dry gourd and save yourself." At once the hornet flew into the gourd – and Anansi plugged the hole with mud.

To capture the python, Anansi cut a stout pole and walked past Onini's house. Speaking loudly to himself, so that Onini could hear, he declared: "My wife is very silly. She says he is shorter but I say he is longer."

"Who are you talking about?" asked Onini.

"Oh! It's only a silly argument I was having with Mrs Anansi. She thinks you are shorter than this pole."

"Well, we can soon find the truth if I lie beside it," replied Onini. But he could not make himself straight enough.

"Let me tie one end of you to the pole," said Anansi. "That should help." And so in this manner, and without realising, Onini was gradually tied to the pole until he could no longer move.

To capture the leopard, Anansi dug a deep pit across a path that Osebo used. He covered the pit with palm leaves. Osebo fell in and cried with terror.

Anansi ran to a log overlooking the pit. "Anansi, help me!" shouted Osebo.

"Tie this rope around you," advised Anansi, as he spun a thick strand of spider's thread. Soon the leopard was entangled in Anansi's web. Anansi hauled him up and took all three captives to Nyame. The price was paid.

This is how Anansi bought ownership of all the world's stories and tales. So, next time you hear a story – remember where it came from.

Wenebojo and Buffalo

This is the story of how Buffalo (the North American Bison) got his great shoulder hump.

Long, long ago, Buffalo did not have a hump. In the summer he would race across the prairie for fun. Fox ran before him and yelled at all the little animals to get out of the way. But the baby birds in their ground nests could not fly yet. They were trampled on and their nests destroyed.

Each time the birds cried out and told Buffalo not to trample on their nests. But he did not listen and kept destroying their babies.

Out for a walk, Wenebojo heard the birds crying. He saw Fox and Buffalo running across the prairie, causing mayhem.

The buffalo was very important to the Plains Indians for food and clothing.

Wenebojo ran ahead and stopped Buffalo and Fox in their tracks. With his spear, he hit Buffalo hard across the shoulders. At once Buffalo hung his head and humped his shoulders, afraid of the spear and expecting that Wenebojo might hit him again.

"You should be ashamed," scolded Wenebojo. "That's right, Buffalo. Hang your head and raise your shoulders. From this day you will always have a hump on your shoulders, and always carry your head low, because of your shame."

Fox slunk away and dug a hole in which to hide. But Wenebojo saw him and said: "You, Fox, will always live in a hole in the ground, for not saving the birds."

And that is why the buffalo has a shoulder hump, and why the fox lives in a hole in the ground.

Brer Rabbit

This famed Uncle Remus story tells how the trickster Brer Rabbit escapes a sticky situation.

Well now, Brer Fox hated how Brer Rabbit was always playing tricks on everybody. So he decided to capture and kill Brer Rabbit and he came up with a plan. He would make a Tar Baby!

Brer Fox mixed some tar with turpentine. He shaped it into the figure of a cute little baby. Then he put a hat on its head and sat it by the road. Later that day Brer Rabbit walked along the road and spotted the little Tar Baby.

The Uncle Remus animal stories were collected from African-Americans by Joel Chandler Harris and published in 1881.

"Well, hello there. How are you feeling this fine day?" he asked. But the Tar Baby just sat there.

"Are you deaf or just rude?" demanded Brer Rabbit, losing his temper. "Take off that hat and say 'How do you do?' or I'm going to give you such a hiding."

Nothing. "I'll learn ya!" Brer Rabbit yelled at the Tar Baby.

Brer Rabbit took a swing at the Tar Baby and his paw stuck in the tar. He hit again and his other paw stuck. Soon his legs, too, were trapped in the tar.

Brer Fox, hiding nearby, quickly arrived. Brer Rabbit gulped. He had to think fast to get out of this sticky problem! "Oh please Brer Fox, please don't throw me into the **briar patch**."

"The briar patch, eh?" said Brer Fox. "I was going to roast you, but it will be better if you are torn to pieces in the briar patch!"

Brer Fox pulled Brer Rabbit off the Tar Baby and flung him into the briar patch. He waited to hear screams of pain, but – silence. Then he heard Brer Rabbit calling: "I was bred and born in a briar patch, Brer Fox. It's my home! Born and bred in a briar patch."

Hare and Tortoise

Aesop's famous fable describes a race between a hare and a tortoise.

Once upon a time there was a hare who boasted how fast he could run. He was forever teasing Tortoise for his slowness. But one day, Tortoise answered back.

"Who do you think you are? I'll not deny you are swift, but even you can be beaten!"

Hare laughed. "Beaten in a race? Not by you, surely?"

Annoyed by Hare's **bragging**, Tortoise accepted the challenge. The animals planned a lengthy course for the race. Next day at dawn, the two rivals stood at the start line, ready to go.

Hare yawned sleepily as Tortoise plodded off slowly. In fact, when Hare saw how slow Tortoise was, he decided to take a nap.

"Take your time, Tortoise!" shouted Hare. "I'll just grab a nap of forty winks and catch you up in a jiffy, old boy."

Much later, Hare suddenly woke – still at the start! He gazed round, looking for Tortoise. The Sun was sinking down towards the horizon. Tortoise, who had been plodding along since morning, was very close to the finish line.

Hare leapt up and bounded at great speed along the course, trailing a cloud of dust. The finish line was in sight! But too late – Tortoise had beaten him. The animals cheered loudly.

Poor Hare! Tired and in disgrace he slumped down. Tortoise came up beside him, smiled widely and remarked: "Listen, Hare, don't brag about your speed. Slow and steady is all you need!"

Aesop was an ancient Greek slave who wrote a collection of stories we know as Aesop's Fables. It is said that he used his cleverness to acquire his freedom and become an adviser to kings.

Gods and Cats

This Chinese myth explains why cats cannot speak, yet humans can.

When the world was a new place, the Gods decided to appoint one group of creatures to make sure that everything ran smoothly – especially by keeping an eye on all other animals.

The Gods selected the thoughtful, wise-looking Cats. The Cats were given the power of speech so that they could talk with the creator Gods. They were told to report regularly to the Gods about how the world was going.

The Cats, however, were simply not interested in the responsibilities given to them by the Gods. They were far happier sleeping beneath the cherry trees and playing with the falling blossoms.

After a while the Gods appeared and called the Cats.

Cats were probably domesticated around 5,300 years ago in China. They helped to keep grain, stored by farmers, free from rats.

"Why have you not reported to us?" they asked.

"Well, keeping an eye on the world is not of great interest to us," said the Cats. "We are happiest asleep, rolling on the grass and chasing butterflies."

The Gods asked the Cats to be more **diligent**. The Cats promised, but did not. On the third occasion this happened, the Cats declared: "To be perfectly honest, we would rather not have this responsibility."

"Very well," said the Gods, "we will ask the Humans." So the Gods took the power of speech from the Cats and gave it to the Humans. From that day, Humans ran the world. Yet the Cats continued to enjoy the delights of sleep, sunshine, scents and play.

The ancient Egyptians loved cats.
They worshipped the goddess
Bastet, who was represented as a cat.

Androclus and the Lion

This account from ancient Rome recalls how a slave and a lion became best friends.

One day in ancient Rome, the crowds were being entertained in the Colosseum. Lions were let loose amongst unarmed slaves, to rip them into pieces. One of the slaves was Androclus of Dacia.

A fearsome lion approached Androclus – and suddenly stopped, wondering what to do. The lion then padded towards the slave, nuzzled his face and licked his hands. Androclus recovered his composure and appeared to recognise the lion. He stroked it, and the spectators applauded and cheered.

The Emperor demanded to know the cause of such a strange event and called the slave to him.

Androclus explained that his master, the **Proconsul** in Africa, was cruel and beat him daily. So Androclus ran away and hid in a cave in the wilderness. Soon afterwards, a lion entered the cave, groaning with pain. One of its paws was wounded and bloody. Androclus was of course terrified. Yet the lion lay down and stretched out its wounded paw.

The Colosseum was the largest amphitheatre (stadium) of the Roman Empire. It hosted gladiator contests, mock sea battles, animal hunts, executions and battle re-enactments.

Androclus gathered enough courage to approach the great beast. He saw a large thorn in its paw, drew this out and cleansed the wound.

From that time, the slave and the lion lived together in the cave, eating the flesh of animals that the lion killed. However, after three long years, Androclus grew tired of such a hard and brutish life. He left and returned to civilisation.

Just three days later, Androclus was captured by Roman soldiers. They returned him to the Proconsul, who condemned him to die in the Colosseum of Rome. The lion, too, had been captured for the same fate.

The Emperor, amazed, freed Androclus and presented the lion to him as a gift.

Afterwards, Androclus was often seen in Rome, leading his lion with nothing but a small leash.

Turtle and Peacock

This is a story from ancient India of how a turtle outwits a greedy hunter.

Turtle and Peacock were great friends. They would meet every day on a river bank. After a drink of water, Peacock danced near the river and displayed his bright plumage for the amusement of his friend.

One day, a hunter caught Peacock and prepared to take him away to the market. The unhappy bird begged his captor: "Please let me say goodbye to my friend, Turtle. It could be the last time we might ever meet."

The hunter agreed. At the river bank, Turtle said to the hunter: "If I give you an expensive present, will you let my friend go?"

Pearls found in fresh water grow inside **mussels**.

"Certainly," answered the hunter. Whereupon Turtle dived into the water and a few seconds later came up with a beautiful pearl. He presented this to the hunter, who immediately released Peacock.

Not long after, the hunter returned. He told Turtle that the price for releasing his friend was not enough. The hunter threatened to catch Peacock again unless he received another pearl. But at Turtle's request, Peacock had already fled.

"Well," said Turtle, "I believe that I can get another pearl just like it. Give it to me and I will dive deep and find an exact match."

The hunter handed over his pearl. Turtle dived into the river – and never returned.

Peacocks are native to India. In Hindu culture Lord Karthikeya, the god of war, rides a peacock.

Mainu the Frog

This is the story of how a frog ended up marrying the daughter of the Sun and Moon.

One day a young man named Kimana decided to marry the daughter of the Sun and Moon. He asked each animal in turn if they could take a letter to heaven with his request. But none of the animals knew how to get there.

At last Mainu the Frog went to Kimana's house, saying he could take the letter to heaven. "A frog?!" exclaimed Kimana. "How can you get to heaven when even those with wings cannot?"

"I know the way and they do not," replied Mainu.

Kimana gave Mainu the letter. The frog hopped away and hid in a well. That night, maidens from heaven climbed down to Earth on a magic web made by the Great Spider. They filled the jugs they were carrying with water from the well. Secretly, Mainu jumped into one of the jugs.

The Maidens climbed back up the web to the House of the Sun and left the jugs. Later Mainu climbed out, put the letter on a table and hid.

When the Sun arrived for a drink of water, he saw the letter and read it. "I, Kimana, a man of Earth, wish to marry your daughter."

Nobody could tell the Sun how the letter got there. So the Sun wrote a reply and again left it on the table. Mainu secretly collected the letter and, when the jugs needed refilling with water, he returned to Earth.

Kimana read the letter and said to Mainu, "The Sun wants a purse of money as a wedding gift. How am I to do this if I cannot get to heaven?"

"I will take the purse for you," said Mainu.

Mainu returned to heaven in the same way and delivered the purse. And so it was arranged for the daughter of the Sun and Moon to descend to Earth. Yet there was nobody to greet her.

"How am I to find my husband if he has not come to greet me?" she wondered.

"I will take you," said Mainu, looking out from the well.

"How can you, a frog, help me?"

"I brought you the letter and the money."

"Then it is you I shall marry," said the daughter and took Mainu to heaven at once. As for Kimana – he still awaits his bride.

The frog is amphibian, which means it can live both in water and on land.

Arion and the Dolphin

This tale recounts how a musician of ancient Greece was saved from drowning by a dolphin.

The renowned **lute** player Arion was returning by ship to his home in Corinth, from the port of Tarentum in southern Italy. He had just attended a musical competition in Sicily, which he had won. The sailors, seeing Arion's prizes of gold and jewels, plotted to kill him and steal the treasure.

"Hurl him into the sea," ordered the captain. "If anybody asks after him, we will say we never saw him fall overboard."

Dionysus, the god of wine, was once captured by pirates. They mistook him for a wealthy prince they could hold for ransom. After the ship set sail, the god used his powers to make vines overgrow the ship. He turned the oars into serpents that terrified the sailors into jumping overboard. But then Dionysus took pity on the sailors. He turned them into dolphins, to spend their lives helping people in peril at sea.

When Arion realised his fate, he begged the sailors that he could play one last song on his lute. The sailors, knowing his reputation as a great musician, agreed. Arion began to play, knowing that dolphins liked the sound of music.

The sailors were moved by his wonderful playing – but not enough to stop them from throwing him overboard. Arion splashed into the sea, where the sailors were sure he would drown.

As Arion hoped, his music attracted a dolphin. The creature saved his life by carrying him all the way to land. But in the end the effort of pulling Arion so far was too much and the poor dolphin died on the beach. In gratitude, Arion had a statue of the dolphin erected on that spot.

White Elephant

In this tale, a kindly elephant wishes only to look after his mother.

There once lived a magnificent and rare White Elephant who had a kind-hearted soul. He lived near a lake by Mount Candorana with his mother, who was aged and blind. White Elephant looked after her with great care. He brought her the best fruits from the forest and cool water from the lake.

One day White Elephant came across a forester who had been lost for days. He carried the forester on his back to a village. From here the forester returned to his home, Benaras.

Soon after the King of Benaras's personal elephant died. The king announced a huge reward for anyone who knew of an elephant magnificent enough to replace it.

The forester guided the king's soldiers to where White Elephant lived. On seeing them, White Elephant knew they had come for him. He realised that if he put up a struggle, many soldiers would be killed. So he decided to go quietly.

At Benaras White Elephant was given his own stables and everything he desired. Yet he neither ate nor drank. The king was informed and went to see him.

"Why are you sulking so?" he asked. "Is it not a great honour to serve your king?"

"I can neither eat nor drink for worrying about my poor mother," replied White Elephant. "She is old and blind and has no one to take care of her."

The king was also kindly. On hearing this, he released White Elephant immediately, to return and care for his mother.

Many years later, after White Elephant had died, the king erected a statue of him by the side of the lake. Every year a fine elephant festival was held here, in memory of such a caring and noble soul.

Elephants in Asia have been used by people for many centuries for war, hunting, transport, and logging.

GLOSSARY

bragging Saying something in a boastful manner.

briar patch A thicket of thorny plants, such as brambles.

diligent Showing great care in one's work or duties.

gourd Plants with hard shells or outer casings. These can be hollowed out to make vessels that hold water, such as a bowl or jug.

lute An early stringed instrument, similar to a guitar.

mussel A shellfish similar to an oyster, found in fresh and salty water.

Proconsul Governor of a province in the ancient Roman Republic.

INDEX